Biblical Prosperity

The Bible Way

Rodney Giles

i

Dedication

To my wife Razia for her unwavering support in my pursuit of God's will and for being an incredible and caring partner. Your love and encouragement mean the world to me.

I am also grateful to our mother, Naseem BiBi Masih Barkat, for her daily prayers and the immense support she has shown me as a servant of God. Your presence and unwavering faith have been a source of strength and inspiration.

To our children, Roshan and Mary, you are truly precious to us, and we consider ourselves immensely blessed to have you in our lives. Your presence brings us joy, and your unique qualities inspire and uplift me every day.

Acknowledgment

I would like to express my heartfelt gratitude to Charles Hellier for his invaluable contribution to my journey in ministry. His guidance and mentorship have played a pivotal role in shaping me into the person and minister I am today.

He graciously took me under his wing and provided me with firsthand experience and teachings on the art of ministry. Working alongside him in an administrative capacity was a privilege that I will always treasure.

CONTENTS

About the Author

Rodney Giles, the Founder of Jubilee Network and Destiny Vision Ministries International. The ministry of Rodney Giles is a manifestation of Kingdom work. Since 1985, Rodney Giles has been actively spreading the gospel and serving the body of Christ through evangelism. His journey began with the establishment of an inner-city church in Lakeland, FL, in collaboration with an Assemblies of God Pastor. In 1990 leading him to enroll in Southeastern Bible College. He is an alumni of the esteemed Dr Gerald Derstines Institute of ministry.

In 1994, Rodney Giles experienced a powerful revival led by Evangelist Rodney Howard Browne, which deeply impacted his life and ministry. Throughout his journey. Served on staff at Christian Retreat in an administrative capacity while traveling weekends as a church evangelist and held various pastoral roles including Director of Volunteer Services and Head of the Prayer Ministry Department. He has also been a Christian Television Network (CTN) guest multiple times and Studied under the tutelage of Pastor Karl D Strader of Carpenter's Home church in Lakeland Florida for eighteen years. He has served on the pastoral staff at the Jim Bakker show.

Rodney is affiliated with Full Gospel Business Men's Fellowship International and a member of United Evangelical churches.

Page Blank Intentionally

Author's Note

This book is the result of decades spent under the guidance of experienced men of God and over 30 years of ministry experience. Its purpose is to shed light on the vital aspects of understanding God's will for your life.

Consider it a reference point, a starting point, for navigating the days that follow when you receive God's call. Above all, let it serve as a reminder that even when support seems lacking in your God-given purpose, you are never alone.

May you find solace in the simplicity of its message, free from excessive embellishments, and may its contents resonate deeply within your heart.

Chapter 1: Knowing Your Calling

A Christian can be defined as an individual who wholeheartedly follows and learns from Jesus Christ, embodying the principles of His teachings. In addition, as true believers in Christ, we follow Christ by exemplifying both orthodoxy—the belief in Jesus' life, death, and resurrection—and orthopraxy—the practice of putting that faith into practice. Nevertheless, when individuals in positions of authority, who openly declare their faith in Jesus Christ, fail to enact the principles of that faith in their actions, it has far-reaching consequences. Primarily when the ethics of Christ are not implemented in policy, the less privileged members of society, such as the poor and working class, are significantly impacted.

As we become a manifestation of God's divine light, we illuminate the path for others to embrace and live according to the principles of His Kingdom. While Jesus frequently referred to His followers' community as the Kingdom of God, Christians in the United States might prefer to refer to it as God's Church. Christians are called to embody the principles of God's Kingdom of heaven in the present world, working towards the establishment of justice, mercy, and peace in an ideal society, as says the Lord's prayers, "Your Kingdom come, Your will be done on earth as it is in heaven." They strive to establish a realm where the values of righteousness and compassion prevail—through the redemptive sacrifice of Jesus Christ

In Romans 10:9-10, Paul emphasizes that the foundation of our salvation lies in both confessing with our mouths that Jesus is Lord and believing in our hearts that God raised Him from the dead. This profound declaration leads to our eternal salvation, as faith in our hearts leads to righteousness, and vocalizing our belief brings about salvation. However, it is important to note that this act of faith and confession serves as the initial step in our Christian journey, marking the beginning of a transformative and ongoing experience. Once you pick up your cross and begin this journey with Him, you are commanded to live your lives under Jesus' instruction.

In Matthew 22:37-38, Jesus highlighted the paramount commandment by stating, "You shall love the Lord your God with all your heart, with all your soul, and with all your mind." In addition, He emphasized the inseparable nature of this commandment by stating that loving one's neighbor as oneself is equally significant. The correlation between loving God and loving others is indisputable, as these two spiritual principles are intrinsically intertwined. Therefore, it becomes evident that loving God without demonstrating love towards our fellow human beings is an impossibility, given the interdependent nature of these divine laws.

Love for God and man can grow cold at times, yet it is the foundation of our faith. We can examine how He emphasized and instructed His followers to live the Kingdom ethics here on Earth by commanding that doing good to one's neighbor is like doing good to Him.

"For I was a stranger, and you did not invite me

in, I needed clothes, and you did not clothe me; I was sick and in prison, and you did not look after me," says the statement. "For I was hungry, and you gave me nothing to eat, and I was thirsty, and you gave me nothing to drink."

They will also respond, "Lord, when did we see you hungry, thirsty, a stranger, in need of clothing, sick, or in prison, and did not help you?" He will respond, "Truly I tell you, whatever you did not do for one of the least of these, you did not do for me."

Jesus discussed health care, economics, housing, food insecurity, prisoners, and poverty in Matthew 25:42–45. Tennessee is plagued by all of these issues and is ranked among the lowest in the nation in all of these areas that support "the least of these." If we are to live out the ethics of the Body of Christ to which he calls us, we must ensure that we are on the side of Jesus when it comes to issues such as mass incarceration, affordable housing, livable wages, food insecurity, and health care, all of which are mentioned in the holy scriptures. The virtues exemplified by Jesus Christ serve as the guiding principles for us as believers, serving as a model to emulate in our lives.

As Christians, we have a divine mandate to share the Gospel across the globe. The essence of the "Good News" in the Bible is the proclamation that the Kingdom of God has arrived, which is the transformative message of the cross. Therefore, we are not truly living out and spreading the Good News of Jesus if we are not bringing the hope and joy of Jesus by being the salt and light of the Earth.

Jesus consistently aligned Himself with the marginalized, the vulnerable, and those burdened by oppression, demonstrating His unwavering support for the poor, the sick, and the oppressed. How can we say we are followers of Jesus Christ and ignore His most fundamental call to action? The authorities in prison must not only concentrate on the beliefs required to enter the church fellowship and, consequently, the Kingdom of God but also practice the precepts Christ commands of us.

During my early years as a Christian, I found

myself in a predicament where I hesitated to respond to God's calling upon my life. As a young minister within a conservative Assembly of God church, I encountered a lack of opportunities for growth and development. While I experienced genuine love and respect from those around me, they struggled to discern God's specific plan for my life. As time passed, I increasingly felt the weight of God's calling upon me, yet I remained uncertain about the subsequent actions I should take. It is important to note that at that particular moment, there were no avenues available within my immediate environment to serve in a ministry capacity.

Despite the presence of numerous seasoned ministers with flourishing ministries, the opportunities for me within the Church were limited. The available positions were primarily in security, maintenance, or housekeeping roles, despite the Church boasting a massive 10,000-seat auditorium and employing around 300 staff members. Remarkably, during that era, our Church was recognized as one of the pioneering mega-churches in the country. It encompassed a retirement center, a 24-hour Christian radio station, a full-time K-12 Christian school, and was frequented by Contemporary Christian music artists. All of these accomplishments were achieved in a city with a population of approximately 100,000 people at that time. The closest I came to preaching in that context was when I volunteered on the church prison staff and occasionally filled in for a friend who conducted meetings at the Church.

I suffered for many years, thinking I was not good enough to be in full-time ministry. It's hard to imagine how overwhelming it must be for a young preacher to try and make a name for himself in a ministry of that size with so much talent around. As a result, my spiritual gifts were suppressed or limited because I didn't want to offend the people around me. In silence, I struggled between being called and being told to wait for God's timing.

Throughout my journey, I consistently heard the words "Wait on God" or "God is still preparing you, be patient." It became evident that those around me were unsure of how to guide a young man like me who expressed a deep longing to be used by God. It seemed that unless one went through the perceived "process of preparation," there was little hope of stepping into ministry. Consequently, I became increasingly self-conscious and developed a complex over time. God called me, yet I lacked a platform to express the gifts entrusted to me.

In response, I made a deliberate and prayerful decision to submit myself to my pastor and faithfully navigate the path God had set before me. I chose to embrace the menial tasks offered to me, turning them into opportunities for ministry. Throughout this process, I remained committed to loving and respecting the church leaders, recognizing that my growth and development were intricately tied to this season of preparation.

This book is dedicated to those who feel a deep calling from God but are unsure how to bring it to fruition. It may seem like the people around you are unaware or indifferent to your personal vision. However,

I want you to know that God has not overlooked you. Your unique story is waiting to be unveiled, and it is time for you to embark on the journey of launching your personal vision.

The purpose of this book is to empower you with the confidence to fulfill everything that God has called you to do. It will guide you on a path that leads to the realization of your God-ordained vision.

Chapter 2: Understanding the Will of God

The call of God on my life has always been a source of deep passion, giving me a sense of purpose and meaning. Once you discover the divine plan that God has ordained for you, it becomes an unwavering anchor that holds you steady, especially during times of great difficulty. It serves as a constant inspiration, propelling you to persevere and never lose hope. I consider myself truly blessed by our Lord Jesus Christ, for He has placed me on a path of righteousness aligned with my passions. It is rare for individuals to be able to say that they are doing what they love, and in that regard, I recognize the abundant blessings bestowed upon me.

With time, I have come to understand that when

things are meant to be, they unfold in accordance with God's perfect timing and under His divine guidance. Perhaps the greatest lesson we learn as human beings is that when we surrender our own plans to Him, God reveals His plan for us. It is through this act of surrender that we can fully embrace His purpose and experience the fulfillment it brings.

Although we possess the freedom to choose our own paths, it is important to recognize that the way of the Lord offers unparalleled peace and clarity. His path is the more excellent way, for He designed us with a specific calling in mind and ordained a precise moment in our lives for its fulfillment. As stated in Jeremiah 29:11, *"For I know the plans I have for you declares the Lord... plans to prosper you and not to harm you, plans to give you hope and a future."* God informed Jeremiah even before your existence took shape within the womb, I already ordained and appointed you to be a prophet to the nations.

Just as God formed Jeremiah with a specific purpose in mind, He has also uniquely shaped you because He has a distinct plan for your life. No one else can fulfill that purpose in the same way that you can. Before stepping into the fullness of God's plan, it is essential to only desire what He has ordained for you. This is because God needs to know He can trust you with the responsibilities accompanying His gifts.

Character and Christian maturity play a significant role when it comes to responding to God's call. They serve as indicators of your readiness to embrace the calling and carry out the tasks that God has entrusted to you.

There are times when God will bless us not because we have great faith or based on merit but because of His mercy and grace. When we prioritize God and make Him our utmost focus, He responds to us in ways that align with our heartfelt desires.

I'm reminded of a time when it was like a wilderness experience. I was sick and tired of not getting results and decided to just have it all out with God and settle it. It's like every area was less than satisfactory, and God appeared to be silent in my life. I cried so much in those days as a result of not seeing any results. Through my tears, I found out that God is not into expressing sympathy. Despite my efforts to connect with God, every opportunity seemed to yield no change. In fact, the more I prayed, the more challenging things appeared to become. It felt as though I was trapped, with the walls closing in on me mentally. Prayer became an act of desperation rather than a source of joy. The deeper I placed my trust in God, the more I felt entrenched in a seemingly endless pit.

However, I eventually realized that the Lord was using these circumstances to reveal aspects of myself that required transformation. He was urging me to confront and address the areas within me that needed to be changed.

If two people visit the same doctor concerning two distinct problems in their bodies, they would not get the same diagnosis and, therefore, require different treatment. It works the same way with God. Two people come to the Lord. One of them may be facing financial problems, while the other may be battling a terminal disease. Jesus has to prescribe treatment to both such individuals. In the first case, He may prescribe 2 Corinthians 9:8, *"And God is able to bless you abundantly, so that in all things at all times, having all that you need, you will abound in every good work."* And also, Ephesians 6:8 *"Because you know that the Lord will reward each one for whatever good they do, whether they are slave or free."*

He then tells this Christian to give above and beyond their normal giving and prescribes meditating on this part of His Word daily until it becomes real to them.

To the next individual, he may give a prescription to go on a three-day fast and attend a healing conference where the focus is praying for the sick.

When I went to God for my problem, I assumed more prayer was needed to solve my problem. However, I found out that's not what God needed me to do. He had prescribed me humility and patience, which would make the required changes in me. However, my pride in myself never accepted that prescription. I spent more time praying, yet prayer was not working at all. God does not want us to be presumptuous about what we think we need. He wants us to do what He has asked us to do. He is much more capable in terms of knowing what we need. Prayer cannot do what giving can do; on the other hand, giving cannot do what only prayer can do. God knows what we need and when we need it.

Despite enjoying my work, I unexpectedly faced a daunting challenge. My workplace advised me to move to a different location, which came as a shock. It was disheartening to realize that the years I had dedicated to my job seemed to be in vain. It was a harsh reality to confront, but I knew I had to remain resilient. What made it even more difficult was that the reason behind my lack of promotion had nothing to do with my qualifications but rather stemmed from their personal insecurities about me. This realization hit me hard, and I couldn't help but wonder, aren't we all created in the image of God? Am I not a child of God? Don't I deserve to sit at the head of the table with my brothers in Arms? All of this led me to think about my past.

Everything I attempted to do failed, and my

relationships were not successful. It felt as if I was worse than a failure, and I didn't know why this was happening to me. A person I knew once told me, "Nothing you do ever amounts to anything," and that stuck with me because it captured my exact thoughts about myself. Some years later, another person said to me, "Your problem is you are not patient enough. You quit things before they can materialize." These encounters served as a launching pad helping to produce a change in my life. I literally saw those experiences as a challenge to prove them wrong. In this process, a discovery was made as my life kept going downhill.

During those moments, I observed that certain actions from my past would resurface in my memory. I would feel remorse for things I had forgotten about and seek forgiveness. Just when I believed I had resolved everything, another issue would arise, and the cycle continued. It felt never-ending, impacting every aspect of my life. I used to consider myself a virtuous person, but the Holy Spirit enlightened me to recognize hidden aspects I had overlooked.

I understood that repentance within me would not happen overnight but would be a gradual process. These deeply rooted issues required a season of sincere repentance. Moreover, I recognized that God's process often unfolds gradually, and it was important to surrender to His timing.

I had to permit God to bring certain things to the surface of my life so that He could address them. This involved walking in humility and allowing myself to be vulnerable before God. For many months, I found myself approaching God in a genuine and authentic way, granting Him the freedom to work in my life as He desired.

If we fail to obey God in the little things in our practical daily lives, it creates a backlog of disobedience, and other issues stem from that. Then that can create problems for other areas of our lives. If you wake up one morning to take a shower only to discover that your bathtub is full of water, what would be the first thing that would come to mind? You would probably think your pipes are clogged, which would require a plumber to come and unclog your pipes. When a buildup occurs over time, water cannot flow freely, and as a result, it does not drain properly on its own. It is wisdom to take care of small problems before they become too big to manage. God wants us to stay on top of our problems, not have our problems on top of us. It's not His will for us to suffer loss, but if we don't heed His warnings, we miss the season to correct those things in time to avoid the problem.

As I navigated through numerous layers of problems, I realized the importance of repentance. These unresolved issues had accumulated and were causing decay. It's similar to being in the presence of someone who hasn't taken a shower - the noticeable physical odor. Likewise, in the spiritual realm, the same principle applies. In my own life, there was a backlog of unresolved issues that hindered me from fully receiving God's blessings. If these issues remained unaddressed, it created a barrier for the Lord to work in my life.

I believed everything was fine and assumed God felt the same. Well, needless to say, my repentance process was transferred to the critical care unit because, at this point, normal repentance was not enough. It was deep-rooted, and there had to be a renunciation of all my old patterns and habits that caused these things to happen in the first place.

During my time in the wilderness, I had a significant dream. In the dream, I saw myself as a farmer diligently planting seeds, hopeful for a fruitful harvest. Each day, I would rise and work hard in the field. However, as time went on, it seemed like my efforts were in vain, and there was no sign of growth. I pondered over this dilemma and eventually realized that there was a reproach on the seeds I had sown. Another thought struck me, revealing that there was also a reproach upon the soil itself. The dream concluded at that point.

After looking at myself up close with the help of the Holy Spirit, I was not happy with anything coming out of my harvest (life) field. It was like a bad crop every season, and suddenly, I had hit a threshold in my pain, and I declared a crop failure in my life. It was my decision to destroy the whole thing and make it new. I knew it would take a lot of work and commitment, but I was determined that I wasn't going to live like this any longer. I was willing to take whatever steps were necessary for God to fix me. I decided to put the new ground in for a new seed time and harvest season. This time, it would require the use of good seeds for my new field.

This dream is indicative of the process of repentance and forgiveness required for me to produce a good harvest. I needed a new approach and new methods for doing things in my life. New ground, new seed, and a new attitude, with pure motives, could help produce the good harvest I needed.

The will of God is ultimately about every believer in Christ operating in their God-ordained place and living free from sin as a way of life. That does not mean perfection, but it does mean we work at it daily to live good clean lives.

Sometimes when your breakthrough is at the door, you can destroy your favor by disobedience in small practical things. If you don't stay in your place, you will not have God's grace, and things will be much harder for you to accomplish.

I remember when Abraham went into battle against King Chedorlaomer and his allies. He won the battle but took nothing from the King's spoils and was submitted to Melchizedek, and this uncommon priest declared Abraham as the servant of the Most High God, who is the Possessor of Heaven and Earth and who takes care of all of Abraham's enemies.

Abraham actually, prior to this great victory, had gone through a season of famine. That season prepared him to win the battle against this huge army of experienced soldiers as well as his entire faith journey.

Living according to God's instructions is the key to biblical prosperity. Biblical prosperity is primarily not about money but about the whole man being blessed to do the will of God. Being submitted to whatever He tells you to do, then your life produces good fruit. Every one of you is uniquely different, and God has a specific road for each of you to travel throughout the course of your life. That road carries a unique set of experiences that are tailor-made for you as an individual. It also carries a certain degree of benefits that are uniquely made for you only.

Then God gives you wisdom for decisions concerning every area of your lives, and He provides ideas and insights for how to prosper and solve problems that might arise from time to time. Biblical prosperity creates an environment for you to thrive. You are blessed as a pattern in place of having problems as the pattern. That is not from your own merits but because of His goodness and mercy.

I rendered null and void things that were not working and started focusing on things I found to be working for me.

1. Acting on the Word of God,
2. Develop a quality prayer life

Making practical decisions through a process of diligence and meditating on the world has produced better decisions. In essence, you are waiting on God meditatively whenever making an important decision because decisions will ultimately determine the direction your life will take. I personally read at least one chapter from Proverbs daily to attract wisdom in my life. The journey towards success, taken step by step, holds greater value than achieving it all at once. Along the way, you can learn from your mistakes and make wiser decisions for your future. Unforeseen challenges become less likely to derail your progress as you gain clarity on what needs to be done and how to do it. By being accountable to the wisdom of God, both you and I increase our chances of success in all endeavors.

I learned the hard way that you don't have to always get your ideas from creating them yourself. I have learned that as a believer in Christ, it's okay to have different ways of doing things in terms of sources and methods. You don't have to be rigid with your approach to getting things done.

Flexibility is like your best friend, and being rigid and inflexible works against what you're doing. It's not always necessary to be right in your own eyes. These things are akin to pride in your lives; in fact, with God, you must be pliable to reach a place where God can use you for His glory. Part of that process is about resisting pride.

Diligence should be applied in anything that we do. The Lord will always select those He finds busy working. You can't sit around waiting for something and expect God to use you. If the Lord has called you to ministry, you should be ministering; if He has called you to be a school teacher, you should be teaching. Whatever He has called you to do, then you should be actively pursuing your assignment. Start where you are, and God will bless your efforts.

Business success in advancing the Kingdom of God requires obedience, being faithful, and being motivated by love for God and people.

Chapter 3: True Giving Produces Bible Prosperity

It is essential to grasp the truth that God desires prosperity for His people. This understanding is rooted in the teachings of the Bible, which affirm God's intention to bless and provide for His children. While biblical prosperity encompasses various aspects of life beyond material wealth, it is vital to have faith in God's willingness to grant abundance.

In 3 John 1:2, we find the apostle John's heartfelt prayer: "Beloved, I pray that you may prosper in all things and be in health, just as your soul prospers." This verse highlights the desire for holistic prosperity, encompassing physical, emotional, and spiritual well-being. God desires our overall success and flourishing.

However, it is crucial to acknowledge that the path to biblical prosperity often involves seasons of testing and refining. In James 1:2-4, James encourages believers to embrace trials, knowing that they produce endurance and shape our character. These testing periods serve to strengthen our faith, refine our motives, and deepen our dependence on God.

Our society is currently under the influence of the top 1%, while the majority of people strive hard to become a part of that wealthy elite. This prevailing system appears to favor those who are already privileged, perpetuating the cycle of generational wealth transfer to their children and grandchildren. Essentially, the same wealth keeps circulating among individuals who have not earned it but inherited it solely due to their family name. Within this system, there is a sense of exploiting one another and displaying contempt toward the less fortunate. It is conceivable that if Jesus were present today, he would likely raise His voice against those who control the global banking system. Their deliberate actions led to the disenfranchisement of everyone except the top 1%, a situation that Jesus would undoubtedly address in His teachings. We can say this because Jesus' parables often challenged societal norms and highlighted the importance of using wealth and resources responsibly. In the parable of the rich man and Lazarus (Luke 16:19-31), Jesus exposed the stark contrast between the opulence of the rich man and the destitution of Lazarus, emphasizing the eternal consequences of neglecting the needs of the poor. Reciprocity is a spiritual law established by God for our own benefit, and it can be activated in our lives at any time. The concept of reciprocity stems from our actions and the corresponding reactions that follow. An excellent example of this principle can be found in the design of most doors, which utilize hinges to allow smooth and free movement. When we open a door, it responds by swinging back in the opposite direction. Similarly, the Bible teaches us that God first demonstrated His love for us by giving His Son to die for our sins. When we respond by accepting His gift of eternal life, we reciprocate His love.

The truth is the extent to which we desire to experience God's blessings and benefits is directly proportional to our practice of reciprocity. The biblical principle of treating others as we would like to be treated encourages us to consistently do good, knowing that goodness will be returned to us in due time.

God's intention is not for us to live in poverty, as it does not align with His purpose for us on Earth. However, accumulating wealth for the sole purpose of personal gain was never part of God's plan either. True prosperity, according to God's desires, is meant to enable us to fulfill His will and bring glory to His name. It is essential that our motives are pure and that our spiritual maturity is developed in order to handle prosperity when it comes our way.

Attaining biblical prosperity necessitates a sustained discipline of giving in accordance with God's guidance and in the places He directs us. By doing so, we open ourselves up to receive God's abundant grace, which meets our needs and empowers us to continue helping others for the sake of His name. While our sacrifices may not be as significant as Abraham's, they still hold great significance in the eyes of our Lord.

Biblical prosperity flourishes as we become

adept at following God's instructions for our individual assignments. It can be said that when God desires to accomplish something, He always has the means to bring it to fruition. Genesis 39 illustrates Joseph's story of how following God's instructions and remaining faithful in difficult circumstances can lead to prosperity and blessings. Despite his setbacks and trials, Joseph's unwavering commitment to God's ways ultimately brought him success and allowed him to fulfill the purpose God had for his life. The Bible has given us a roadmap for biblical prosperity as a way of life.

When we give our tithes, we not only honor God with what rightfully belongs to Him, but we also acknowledge that He is our ultimate source. The concept of tithing involves giving 10% of our income or resources back to God. It is important for us, as Christians, to grasp the understanding that what we may consider as our own possessions actually belong to God. Our money, material resources, and even our very lives have been graciously given to us by God. It is crucial to recognize that everything we possess is temporary and fleeting. Therefore, we should cultivate an attitude of gratitude, avoiding the pitfalls of pride and arrogance. In the presence of the almighty God, we are but insignificant specks of dust, and it is through humble gratitude that we can maintain the right relationship with Him.

Imagine your neighbor has a bountiful garden and decides to generously gift you twenty ears of corn. In this scenario, it is important to remember that even though the corn is given to you, two ears actually belong to God. You are entrusted with the remaining 90% for your own use. This serves as a reminder that, ultimately, everything belongs to God. Understanding this fundamental truth is crucial.

Tithing is not about us assisting or providing for God, as if He were in need of anything from us. Instead, it is a means through which God blesses our lives by granting us what we truly need. Tithing is also linked to our attitudes and beliefs regarding the origin of our possessions. Recognizing that everything comes from God helps us cultivate an appreciative and grateful mindset.

Tithing is rooted in the belief that 10% of our possessions do not belong to us but rather represent a test of our faithfulness and discipline. It serves as a tangible expression of our love for God, demonstrating our commitment to Him.

Before giving our tithe, it is an act of Worship to offer gratitude and praise to God for His abundant blessings in our lives. Tithing is a reflection of our acknowledgment of past blessings, recognizing that it is God who has provided for us.

It also serves as a protective measure, safeguarding us from financial loss and unforeseen challenges. When we prioritize giving the tenth to God first, He blesses the remaining ninety percent to fulfill its intended purpose. Often, unexpected expenses arise that require us to dip into our savings. However, when we faithfully tithe, unexpected blessings find their way into our lives, replenishing what we may have used in times of need. Tithing plays a vital role in cultivating a life of blessings and abundance. Tithing plays a significant role in experiencing a life filled with God's blessings.

In the book of Malachi in the Old Testament 3:10, God challenges His people to bring the full tithe into the storehouse and promises to pour out blessings in abundance. It states: "Bring the full tithe into the storehouse, that there may be food in my house. And thereby put me to the test, says the Lord of hosts, if I will not open the windows of heaven for you and pour down for you a blessing until there is no more need." Here, God encourages His people to faithfully bring their tithes, assuring them that He will bless them abundantly. This verse exemplifies the belief that tithing is a test of faithfulness and discipline, where God promises to reward His people for their obedience by pouring out blessings from heaven.

Giving offerings is another way of demonstrating our love for God and expressing gratitude. Offerings are a way for us to express gratitude to God and show our faith with hopeful expectations of His future blessings. They represent the things we anticipate receiving but have not yet obtained. Giving offerings goes beyond our obligation and tests our faith. They symbolize our willingness to give up something dear to us out of love for our Lord. Compared to the immense sacrifice of Jesus on the cross, our offerings are a small token of appreciation.

Unlike tithes, which already belong to God, offerings are solely based on our voluntary choice to give. They mark the beginning of true generosity. Typically, offerings are designated for various church projects such as building funds, ministry vehicles, and other additional needs.

Then we have Almsgiving, a form of giving dedicated solely to the support of the less fortunate. It encompasses providing essentials such as food, clothing, and other necessities for those who are in need. Generously giving to the poor without seeking recognition or praise holds a special significance in the eyes of God. In Christianity, it is a fundamental principle to offer assistance selflessly without expecting anything in return, not even gratitude. However, it is essential to remember that God observes not only the act of giving but also the intentions and sincerity of the giver, as well as the quality of the gift.

The first fruit offering holds a special place in my heart as a personal act of gratitude, although it is not specifically commanded by Jesus. It is a voluntary gift that reflects the concept of giving to God from the very beginning of our blessings. An illustration of this can be found in the story of Cain and Abel, where both individuals offered gifts to God but with different outcomes. Cain presented an offering from his ordinary crops, while Abel offered the finest and firstborn of his flock, along with the fat portions. This account highlights the thoughtfulness behind Abel's offering and suggests his superior attitude toward the gift. Abel prepared a gift that was befitting to honor a King, showcasing his respect for God and acknowledging His ownership over all things.

The first fruit offering presents a unique opportunity to initiate a blessed life. Personally, I attribute this offering to my journey of transforming from a state of indebtedness to achieving financial freedom. Whenever I have honored this offering with reverence, God has consistently blessed me in remarkable ways. If you find yourself struggling with debt and unable to break free, I challenge you to embark on a sustained practice of giving your first fruits, and you will witness a season of abundant blessings in your life.

Chapter 4:
Understanding Our
Purpose and the
Leadership of Christ

What are we doing in this wilderness? What are we trying to seek? Is it the glory of Christ? These are only a few questions that are central to all our lives. Questions like, "Where are we? Where are we going? And where will we end up? These questions are at the heart of every human being, but sadly, we have drifted away from our faith which has led us astray and kept us on a path that has but only one end. So the question is, where do we go in this wasteland in search of our better selves?

In today's world, a leadership void needs to be filled desperately, particularly in the body of Christ.

Unfortunately, we don't have the skills of leadership required for the set of problems or issues people are facing in today's world. An unfortunate example of the prevailing circumstances is the assault on the truth that has gained prominence in the past five years. Our political landscape is in disarray, and it is crucial for leaders to unite and address these challenges both within our nation and globally, speaking with a unified voice. The media, politics, and religious institutions have lost their way, and our country has become completely divided. These institutions have become part of the problem, and so many are influenced by them that most people have become lost in it all. I hate to say this, but it's as if we have lost our collective vision as a nation. Every party has its own agenda, and yet they are both parts of the same side of the evil coin. These institutions pretend to be for the truth but openly work for their self-interest, which includes the power and influence associated with the US dollar. They have sold their morals, principles, and, most importantly, their souls.

A significant issue we face is that many

individuals are not aligned with their life's purpose. God has bestowed upon each of us a unique calling to fulfill in our lives, but unfortunately, most find themselves on a divergent path. If each person would simply be laser-focused on what God has called them to do, that would be half of the solution.

Leadership, to a certain degree, must be up to everyone. Being a leader doesn't mean dominating others or ruling by fear, but it's about attracting people to follow you because of the gift that God has placed in you to get things done for His glory. It's about being confident when others are feeling uncertain about which course to take. Many people don't have a purpose, and hence you see the state of the country where people don't even know themselves, let alone God. They have become wayward, so much so that the churches that should be the solution are failing the people.

If we all really believed that the return of Jesus Christ was imminent, we would respect the Ten Commandments again. I suspect that we would all read our Bibles and walk in harmony with the laws of God.

Yet we deny Him and make ourselves busy and wander in the nothingness of this materialistic world. If we truly believed, we would try to live clean lives and be people of integrity. However, the good news is that it's never too late, as now is the time to find what the Lord has for you. In all my years of trial and trying to succeed, I was able to glean some things from those experiences. My failures and setbacks had to do with changes that were needed in me.

There are three main reasons that helped me understand why I felt stuck.

Reason 1:

Firstly, during a season of spiritual testing, I realized I was impatience. I wanted instant results and tried to achieve things on my own strength. However, I learned that God's timing is crucial in fulfilling His will. Every time I rushed into something, it ended in failure because I didn't have the patience to learn and wait for the right season.

What did it remind me of?

It reminds me of King Saul, who was instructed to wait for Samuel before offering a sacrifice to God. Saul grew anxious when Samuel was delayed and acted impulsively by making the sacrifice himself. Just as Saul realized his mistake, Samuel arrived and reminded him that obedience was more important than sacrifice.

What did I learn from it?

Our actions for God should align with His timing and be motivated by the guidance of the Holy Spirit.

Reason 2:

In the second season, when I went through a spiritual test, I discovered that I was prideful as the old saying goes my way or the highway. Things had to be my way, whether in relationships or anything else.

What was I reminded of?

I was reminded of an experience with a work situation many years ago. I was starting a job that I had previous experience with, and some of my co-workers attempted to train me on better techniques to be more efficient. I was offended by them giving me advice considering my previous experience and background. My first thought was, how dare they try to train me on this job that I have done for years? What I missed was they were not trying to train me. They were simply trying to show me a better way of doing things to save me time and effort.

What did I learn from it?

I learned through that season that we should be willing to have better methods and not be fixed with just one way of doing things. You can't make your vision a reality all by yourself. It's important to be open to accepting help from others who can contribute to bringing your vision to life. Your attitude is key because it can either attract the right people who want to support you or push them away. So, stay positive and friendly to create a welcoming environment for those who can help you on your journey.

Reason 3:

The third spiritual test revealed that I needed to

have pure motives for everything I did for God. Motives cannot be based on things that are dishonest or out of self-interest. It must be rooted in obedience and based on biblical love.

What was I reminded of?

It reminded me of Saul's battle against the Amalekites (1 Samuel 15:1-23). God commanded Saul to completely destroy the Amalekites and all their possessions as a result of their wickedness. However, Saul and his army spared the best of the livestock and goods, intending to keep them for themselves. When Samuel, the prophet and judge, confronted Saul about his disobedience, Saul claimed that he had kept the livestock to offer sacrifices to God. Samuel reminded Saul that God valued obedience over sacrifices and informed him that God had rejected him as king due to his disobedience.

What did I learn from it?

In order to succeed in doing the will of God, there has to be a degree of flexibility with us in terms of methods. God cannot use us if we are unteachable; we must be pliable and allow Him to be the Savior and Lord of our lives.

When it comes to principles, it's important to stand firm and stay unwavering. Being dedicated to following God's will for our lives brings a sense of centeredness and focus. When you realize that your calling is intertwined with your life's purpose, you discover where your true value, joy, and peace lie. In fact, everything you want, desire, and need can be found within God's plan for your life.

Kingdom relationships come about as a result of stepping into your God-ordained purpose. God has not called you to do it alone. There are people called to stand alongside you to do His will. Recall Moses and Aaron. When God called Moses, He specifically mentioned, *"What about your brother, Aaron the Levite? I know he can speak well. He is already on his way to meet you, and he will be glad to see you"* Exodus 4:14.

Divine connections create opportunities to get things done for God without having to break doors down or reinvent the wheel. People can give you material things as well as gifts, talents, and abilities you need to fulfill your purpose in life.

Divine favor is a grace that comes into our life when we are in our place and walking in obedience. I found out that favor is consistently working for us as we pursue the plan of God with no other agenda in mind. Favor works on our behalf. For example, we might need a good car because what God has called us to do requires travel. Then let's say we don't have the money to buy a new car at that particular time. Perhaps our finances are stretched too thin, and perhaps even our credit would not allow us to get a loan. God is telling us to do something that we can't do. However, we simply decide to start where we are without the new car in our possession. God has the power to bring someone into our life who can play a significant role, much like Boaz did for Ruth. When we obediently follow God's guidance, we provide Him with an opportunity to work in our favor and bring positive outcomes to our situation. Our act of obedience becomes a catalyst for God's intervention and the manifestation of His favor. Once we understand that every good thing comes from God, then we will be thankful and follow the pathway he has set for us.

Divine health comes about when the life of God and the health of God permeate our very being. God can sustain our body with the power of the Holy Spirit daily. God's kind of health makes it physically possible to do the will of God. If God has called us to a traveling ministry, for example, then that requires having good health. Moses, at 80 years old, was called to lead the children of Israel out of Egypt. He was not exactly a young man at the time. They ended up spending 40 years in the wilderness. We see that in all that time, God kept them in good health. The Bible says that Moses' eyes were not dim, nor was his natural force abated in all his life. If we are diligent in prioritizing God's Kingdom in our lives, we will also witness positive outcomes in our physical well-being.

In simple terms, every person wants to be healthy and have a peaceful mind in their daily lives. Real prosperity doesn't come from money but from the everlasting security provided by the cross. This should always be the focus of our faith. It means aligning ourselves with God's laws and following Jesus' commandments in our everyday lives.

On a human level, we can all agree that everyone wants to understand their purpose in life. As human beings, the key to consistently living a blessed life is to prioritize spiritual matters above everything else. Other aspects of life should take a back seat in comparison.

Jesus encouraged His followers not to be overly concerned about material needs such as food, drink, and clothing. Instead, he advised us to prioritize seeking God's Kingdom and righteousness above all else. By putting God first, we can trust that our basic needs will be taken care of. This illustrates the importance of aligning with spiritual values and trusting in God's provision. The idea of prioritizing spiritual matters above everything else is found in the Gospel of Matthew, chapter 6, verses 31-33: *"So do not worry, saying, 'What shall we eat?' or 'What shall we drink?' or 'What shall we wear?' For the pagans run after all these things, and your heavenly Father knows that you need them. But seek first His Kingdom and His righteousness, and all these things will be given to you as well."*

So, in conclusion, we must capture the vision God has given us from within ourselves. Then we must depend upon Him to manifest that vision so that others, i.e., the nation, can be blessed as a result.

Chapter 5: Praying in the Will of God

Prayer is the source of fulfilling God's will for our life. God is interested in talking to us daily. He is the friend we need when everything and everyone else has abandoned us. He will be there even if we do not believe in Him.

The disciples asked Jesus how to pray, and He gave them a complete formula. A way of being, a way to communicate with the Almighty, a connection that has no boundaries and is vast beyond whatever we can imagine.

This formula taught us how to prioritize our prayer to God. Prayer is literally the foundation for all believers to be successful in terms of practical life. It will give us the kind of peace most people spend their entire lifetime searching for and yet never find, even though it's right in front of them.

This formula works for all, the poor, the rich, the hungry, the sick, and the healthy, and most importantly, it doesn't take too much time or ask for a lot, just that we have love in our hearts. To Oswald Chambers, "Worship and intercession must go together; the one is impossible without the other. Intercession involves actively seeking the mind of Christ as you pray for someone, stirring yourselves to align with His perspective concerning that individual."

Jesus often went away to be alone with His Father in prayer, but the Bible does not go into any details concerning what He prayed. If His teachings were any indication, we could assume that Jesus spent more time listening to His Father's voice than talking about His needs, wants, and desires. It is very typical for the average Christian to spend their prayer time asking for things from God rather than asking God what He wants from them. If we ask God what He wants, that will require us to listen in order to get the answer. Wanting things lies in the very nature of humans. A lot of people talk to God when they are in need, but I believe we should communicate with God even if we are not in need, fostering a constant connection and relationship with Him.

God is a gentleman. He will speak to us in a quiet place and when we become quiet. Meaning prayer is a sacred thing and a unique relationship between God and us and needs to be protected and not flaunted in any way.

There are a few things we can do that will keep us on the road to an effective prayer life.

Psalm 100:4 says that we should "*enter His gates with thanksgiving and into His courts with praise.*"

i. We are to ask God for the things that we need and trust Him to provide them for us.
ii. We are to forgive everyone as an automatic response that is the condition of blessing. We must forgive no matter the offense.
iii. We are to be full of prayer, full of the Holy Ghost, and full of the Word of God and full of fruitful works. Then when our obedience is fulfilled, we

pray that God will keep us from evil and that we are not grieved as we live for him.

iv. Make Him your only need, and He will answer our prayer before we ask Him, and while we are speaking, He will hear us. Even when we intercede on behalf of another, God can help the person because He honors our righteous prayer. James 5:16 says, *"The prayer of a righteous person has great power as it is working."*

v. We should not come before our King empty-handed but bring an acceptable offering before the Lord; our bodies should also be a holy sacrifice unto the Lord. We are to worship God and make Him our King in prayer.

Now, you may wonder what it truly means to make God our King.

It entails surrendering everything to Him, including our very lives. We prioritize seeking His presence and advancing His Kingdom above all else, making His righteousness our primary focus.

Furthermore, we align our material giving with the initial sacrifice of surrendering our lives to Him. Scripture instructs us to honor our King first when it comes to financial priorities.

Then His righteousness is a life pursuit, and it says that all these things (our needs, etc.) will be added as a gift. That is not a wage-based system which means we are doing work to receive those blessings.

The Gentiles or unbeliever is earning it, but the believer in Christ will get it from their King, who provides all things for us to enjoy richly. It's a process to walk this out, but when we understand it, then it comes consistently as a gift to us.

The essence of the Kingdom of God lies in acknowledging God as our King, and as His children, we have the privilege of being part of His Kingdom. It is the most desirable place for us to be. In a kingdom, the King possesses everything. Unfortunately, the topic of prosperity in the mainstream Church has often revolved around self-centeredness. However, our Heavenly Father graciously provides for us to enjoy the blessings of prosperity within His Kingdom.

The Babylonian or worldly system operates on the principle of pursuing personal gain and accumulating as much as possible without concern for others. In contrast, the Kingdom system revolves around acknowledging God as our King, which brings about a completely different perspective. Within this paradigm, we understand that everything we have belongs to God by His rightful authority as our King. Personally, I believe that God is eagerly waiting to bless individuals who would simply acknowledge Him as their King.

We are to pray scriptural prayers before God because He only recognizes the Word of God. As previously stated, the average person comes before God about their needs. In fact, many can't occupy 30 minutes with God without running out of things to pray about. It's not the amount of time that matters as much as it is about the quality of time. There are times when we need one hour with the Lord, and most of that should be spent listening to His voice.

Did you know that most of what we discuss with

God in prayer is not as important as what He has to say to us? It's true we must come to get direction from our King in terms of advancing His Kingdom. Also, developing our intimacy with God as a way of life. He loves us and desires to have an intimate relationship with us. We give the Lord the first part of our day and discuss with Him things that are on the heart of God.

There are things to discuss regarding expanding the Kingdom of God on Earth. Each of us has a part to play in that, and we want to understand His plan for our part. We must see the meeting of our needs being fulfilled as something connected to God's plan. In other words, God gives us things to use for His plan for our life. Because in the Kingdom, it's all about Him as King; we are simply His citizens.

Praying in other tounges, aka our heavenly prayer language, will edify our spirit and download supernatural answers. This form of prayer provides us with a direct communication line to God. Jude 1:20 says, *"But ye, beloved, building up yourselves on your most holy faith, praying in the Holy Ghost."*

Chapter 6: Finances for the End Times

As the old saying goes, there is only one guarantee in life which is death. It's something that will come to us all, no matter how much we try to run from it. This leads to many among us having an existential crisis knowing that our time on Earth is limited. While life is undeniably precious, its true value lies in living it purposefully, free from worldly distractions and personal desires. Therefore, we must introspect and ask ourselves a fundamental question: Are we living to fulfill our own desires or to align ourselves with a higher power, such as God?

God has been preparing us over time for things that are to come upon the Earth. Everyone living on this Earth will make their transition sooner or later should the Lord tarry His coming. According to the Bible, we are encouraged to diligently use our time and resources until the arrival of God's Kingdom. This involves prioritizing His divine purpose for our lives. However, to fulfill His will, we require financial means. As citizens of His Kingdom, we must view ourselves as more than what we currently are. In fact, God's plan for us is so immense that we cannot accomplish it without His assistance.

God has placed a personal vision within us that has to be discovered. In essence, each of us has a unique and meaningful purpose to fulfill during our time on Earth. God has equipped us with the necessary resources to accomplish it. However, this purpose is intricately tied to our willingness to embrace and pursue our vision with boldness and action.

Kingdom people will have to see themselves other than somebody's employee or simply being wage earners. In these end times, believers in Christ will have to own businesses and be good stewards of the time and resources that God provides. This is so that God's plan can be completely paid for with more than enough to help others that might be in need. God will look for those who work honestly on their job. During their scheduled work hours, diligent employees focus on their work and refrain from stealing or deceiving their employer. God values individuals who exhibit an exemplary work ethic and willingly go beyond their job requirements. By adopting a problem-solving mindset and striving to bring value to their employer, individuals can gain the necessary skills and experience to potentially become entrepreneurs in the future.

Now is the time to stop and think about changes that we can make in our lifestyles. There may be an opportunity to cancel subscriptions that we don't need. Maybe trim our social budget down or perhaps eat less often than we are used to eating. Because we will need this money for the plan of God

In order to swiftly attain financial freedom and be available to serve God and fulfill His purposes, it is crucial to prioritize debt repayment and diligently keep track of our expenses through proper record-keeping. By doing so, we can remove the burden of debt and create the necessary space to dedicate ourselves wholeheartedly to His service. There are people working for someone else, but God has called them to start a business. In the last few days, everyone will need to be in the place that God has decided for them to get everything God has for them to accomplish. Everything is about Kingdom's vision and then the finances to accomplish and realize that vision. We need to remember that we will leave this Earth taking nothing, not even our bodies, so why do we spend extravagantly on things that are outside of our needs?

A vital aspect of serving God involves the willingness to distribute resources as He directs in order to fulfill His plans. It is important to recognize that everything we possess, including our homes, cars, and finances, ultimately belongs to God.

There might come a time when God will call on us to give something away that we currently value. In the Kingdom, nothing is ours. It all belongs to the King, and in His Kingdom, He can take anything He needs because it legally belongs to Him. We must understand this point because everything else is connected to this one spring.

We have been conditioned to the Babylonian system. God says that we are not to love the world or anything in the world, which means that we are to reject the world's way of doing things.

In other words, we need a new mentality to obey God for end-time purposes. We see the King and His plans as a priority, and God will manifest them through His people. The work of God will have to be financed by believers with money.

The possessions and resources bestowed upon us by God are not intended for selfish accumulation or personal enjoyment alone. Rather, they are entrusted to us for the purpose of carrying out His will. When God blesses us with something, He trusts us to use it wisely and appropriately, ensuring it reaches the intended recipients at the appointed time.

In the times ahead, our attachment should solely be to our King, recognizing that everything ultimately belongs to Him. We will be held accountable to God for how we manage and steward His resources. The body of Christ needs to seek divine wisdom in order to fulfill

God's plan on Earth.

Chapter 7: Faithful Stewardship - Unveiling the Rewards of Tithing

And here men that die receive tithes; but there he receiveth them, of whom it is witnessed that he liveth. (Hebrew 7:8)

Throughout the Old Testament, tithing is mentioned, particularly when God gave the Israeli tribe of Levi the task of taking care of the Tabernacle and serving as spiritual leaders for the nation of Israel. God instructed the rest of the Israelites to bring tithes of their increase to provide for the priests and Levites because the tribe of Levi was given these two distinct duties and did not receive a portion of land, as He had done with the other tribes of Israel, Joshua 13:14.

Jesus affirmed the practice of tithing in the New Testament (Matthew 23:23), and the Apostle Paul urged

Christians to give to those in need and those who were sharing the Gospel (II Corinthians 9:6–15). By giving today, we make it possible for those whom God has called to serve as pastors, missionaries, and ministry staff to faithfully build up the Church and expand God's Kingdom.

Let us have a look at the various facets of the tithes:

1. **Put It into Practice**

   One way to worship God is to tithe, which is a way to acknowledge that God is our provider and to remind ourselves that all our resources are His and come from His grace. When we choose to offer God ten percent of our income, we set a course for how we will handle the rest of our money to honor God.

2. **When to Give:**

   To establish a consistent giving pattern, it is important to consider our pay schedule and allocate funds accordingly. By doing so, we not only honor God's faithfulness in providing for but also demonstrate our gratitude by generously meeting the needs of others. Regular giving can become a habit that reminds us of God's blessings and encourages us to continue sharing with those around us.

3. **Whom to give:**

As a general guideline, it is recommended to allocate the tithe, which is ten percent of our income, however Tithes belong to God not the pastor and ultimately its up to God where to sow your tithe to the Church we regularly attend. Our pastor and ministry staff members are supported by these donations, which also contribute to the upkeep of the Church's work in our community. Additional gifts can be given to other ministries that are advancing the Gospel as God directs and prospers us.

4. **How much to give:**

The tithe equals ten percent of our net income. We must also consider tithing other resources, such as our time (giving Him the first part of your day in quiet time and dedicating one day in seven to worship and rest), as well as our energies (investing your talents and skills in our Church and community). This is in addition to giving God 10% of our monetary income.

5. How to Give:

God values our reasons for giving. Let each person give according to his or her heart's desire, voluntarily or out of necessity: God loves generous people, after all. Furthermore, God can shower us with all grace, that "ye may abound to every good work, always having all sufficiency in all things" (II Corinthians 9:7–8). Give knowing that God will always provide for our every need so that we can do more good deeds!

6. Why Should we give tithe?

Tithing plays a crucial role in developing a reverent fear of God. Tithing serves as a perpetual reminder of our reliance on God's provision and care. It provides an opportunity to express our gratitude for all His blessings during prosperous times and instills in us a constant awareness of His role as our ultimate source of provision.

Tithing also encourages us to trust in God's ability to meet all our needs and to recall His faithfulness in challenging times. By faithfully tithing, we develop a deeper sense of gratitude, trust, and dependence on God, which ultimately strengthens our relationship with Him.

In Deuteronomy 14:22–23, God gave the Israelites these instructions: True tithing is required for all of your seed's harvest. Of your corn, wine, and oil, as well as the firstlings of your herds and flocks, so that you can learn to always fear the Lord your God. Tithing is an important part of learning to live in God's fear, no matter where you are right now; invest in Heavenly treasures as Christians because we are urged to focus on the things that truly matter, not the frivolous things of this world as Paul says in the letter to the Colossians 3:2, *"Set your minds on things above, not on earthly things."* Even Jesus warned His disciples and commanded us in Matthew 6:19–21, *"Lay not up for yourselves treasures upon earth, where moth and rust doth corrupt, and where thieves break through and steal: But lay up for yourselves treasures in heaven, where neither moth nor rust doth corrupt, and where thieves do not break through nor steal: For where your treasure is, there will your heart be also."*

3 Malachi: 10-12 says, *"Bring ye all the tithes into the storehouse, that there may be meat in mine house, and prove me now herewith, saith the Lord of hosts if I will not open you the windows of heaven, and pour you out a blessing, that there shall not be room enough to receive it. And I will rebuke the devourer for your sakes, and he shall not destroy the fruits of your ground; neither shall your vine cast her fruit before the time in the field, saith the Lord of hosts. And all nations shall call you blessed: for ye shall be a delightsome land, saith the Lord of hosts.*

The law of tithing is one of the laws that cannot be changed in order to receive tangible blessings from the LORD. God asks us to sow our tithe—one-tenth of our earnings—as a seed for eternal open heaven blessings out of His generosity. God has provided us with numerous blessings through His creation. Tithing has a supernatural quality to it; everyone who followed the tithing principle in ancient and modern history received multiple blessings at the same time. Tithing is a part of our spiritual worship, Biblical obligation, and stewardship, regardless of the argument against it. God is not avaricious. The majority of business transactions always use a 50/50 sharing formula. But God asked us to give one-tenth of our income as evidence of our faith, thanksgiving, worship, and stewardship because He was generous and wanted to bless us.

God promises ten blessings by tithing, a single act of obedience.

1. It lets you demonstrate that God is your SOURCE.
2. It lets you demonstrate your faith That God will bless the remaining 90% to go further than expected.
3. God promises to open heaven's doors to you.
4. You will be blessed with money and with what money cannot accomplish.

5. There won't be room enough to take in all the blessings.

6. For your benefit, God will REBUKE DEVOURERS.

7. Your harvests will not be destroyed by devourers or parasites.

8. There won't be any mishaps or losses, and neither will your vines produce fruit before the time is up.

9. You will be hailed as blessed by all nations.

10. You will be a blessed person for a witness that God is with you.

Tithing is considered important if you desire God's involvement in your finances. According to God's words, when you give a tenth of your income, you create space for more blessings to flow into your life. The principle of giving and receiving is a fundamental aspect of human existence, seen in concepts such as supply and demand, planting and harvesting, sowing and reaping, and so on. In relation to these principles, neutrality is not possible. Take, for example, the Dead Sea in Israel, which only takes in water and never gives any out, resulting in its lifeless state and apt name.

Consistently giving our offerings provides us with an ideal opportunity to demonstrate our faith in God and witness His provision in our finances. It is crucial to remember that adhering to biblical principles and faithfully tithing brings forth abundant blessings. By placing our hopeful expectations in God's provision, we open ourselves to tenfold blessings promised in His Word.

When we demonstrate unwavering faith in God, the Holy One, He faithfully upholds His covenant promises in our lives. It is important not to let the devil deceive us into withholding our tithe, as our tithe seed acts as protection against lack and insufficiency. By sowing our tithe seed as a covenant seed of Abraham, we position ourselves to experience God's abundant and gracious blessings.

Let us Pray! *"Father, I believe what You say. Because You are the entire source of my supply, I honor You with my tithe. Only You are great enough to satisfy all of my requirements. I give You my tithe with high hopes for the ten blessings that You promised with tithing. Rebuke the devourers on my behalf, Father. I invoke Jesus' blood over my possessions. I will always give my tithe with an optimistic outlook. Amen. "*

Modeling the blessed life is a necessary part of a believer's life in Christ. I always wondered, as a young minister of God, how we could get people excited enough that they would want to serve God. The Bible says that all believers should share the good news about Christ. It says that he that wins souls is wise and that it is our duty to make disciples. The question I had was, how can we win people to Jesus Christ? After all, it was quite an intimidating task to share the message of the cross with people. Many thoughts go through our minds when dealing with unbelievers about this topic. There can be even an element of fear, and It seemed that there had to be a formula for succeeding. As a young minister in those days, I would pray and ask God how to be successful in winning disciples for His glory.

While sharing the message of salvation, I

encountered a range of responses and outcomes. Many people would join in prayer, commonly known as the "sinners' prayer," out of fear, driven by the desire to avoid hell. It became apparent that numerous individuals embraced Christ for this reason alone. However, I found myself unsatisfied with the notion that people serve God only to secure eternal life after death. My desire was to witness their genuine enthusiasm for serving God, fueled by a profound revelation of His love for them and a recognition that following Christ is the superior choice over worldly pursuits.

God revealed something to me about that aspect of serving him. I saw that when we live in obedience to the laws of God, there is a response from Him in terms of practical Christian living. For example, when we give a tithe in the correct way, God promises a response from heaven to our tithe. Tithing is a law in the Kingdom of God, and when we follow that law, something good happens to us.

When we go beyond tithing and giving offerings, we experience a remarkable transformation that exceeds the standard level of giving. While tithing is our obligation to the Kingdom, offerings stem from our voluntary desire to do something beyond what is expected. In essence, it becomes a measure of our love for God. Scripture affirms that the extent to which we give in this manner determines the measure by which God will bless us in return.

So many Christian leaders have used the message of prosperity in a misguided way, and that's unfortunate. Biblical prosperity is a result of faithfully obeying the laws. Blessings come as a natural result of our obedience to God, not for the purpose of accumulating personal wealth but rather to fulfill His covenant on Earth. It is important to recognize that God has a unique and specific assignment for each individual in this lifetime. Before we depart from this world, He desires us to fulfill that assignment. One aspect I can confidently share about your specific assignment is that you are called to proclaim the victory of Jesus Christ and actively participate in making disciples.

God has given us all a way to do that quite

effectively. I found out over the years that we have to offer the world something more than they already have. Deep down, many individuals find themselves lacking genuine inner happiness. They embark on a quest to fill a void within, longing for something more in life. That missing piece is often found in a relationship with Jesus Christ. However, it is not solely the Jesus who offers eternal life that they are missing, but also the understanding of their life's purpose. They yearn to comprehend the reason for their existence, the very purpose for which they were born.

Through my personal journey, the Lord has revealed two significant truths to me. Firstly, when we wholeheartedly follow Him by obeying His Word, He graciously pours out His blessings upon us. Secondly, God has a specific purpose for each of us to fulfill, and accomplishing that assignment requires resources. Therefore, God desires to bless you and me, enabling us to carry out the very purpose He designed us for in life.

One additional reason is that God desires to use us to make other people jealous so they will want to serve

God. When people witness the blessed life we lead in the Kingdom of God, it becomes part of the good news of the gospel. Jesus Christ came to save sinners and restore them to their original purpose for which they were created. Our responsibility is to share the story of His sacrificial death on the cross, reconciling mankind with God. Moreover, we are called to reveal the beauty and reality of living in the Kingdom of God.

The evidence of this transformative life should be evident as we model a blessed existence, free from sorrow, to the world. By embracing and living out the blessings that come from following God's plan, we have the opportunity to lead others to Christ. Through our own lives, we can demonstrate the transformative power of the Kingdom, motivating others to seek the same blessings. It is our purpose to live a life of continual blessings, and this should provoke others to envy and desire the same for themselves. In this way, we can effectively impact the world with the message of the gospel, bringing glory to Christ.

Chapter 8:
Understanding Biblical
Prosperity

There has been erroneous teaching over the years concerning this subject. The Bible talks about how Jesus, who was rich, became poor so that we might be made rich. Jesus also stated, *"I have come that they might have life and that they might have it more abundantly."* Like everything that is good, it originated from God, and the devil has taken a counterfeit and used it in the world. In fact, he used it to tempt Jesus in the wilderness, and he is using it today to tempt us. In the beginning, it was God's will for man to prosper. God put everything in the garden for Adam and called it good. Even there was gold throughout the entire land of Havilah, which was located near the Garden of Eden. Adam was to be the protector of everything in the garden. But Lucifer used deception to get control of the Earth, including the gold. He then turned what was pure into something that became corrupted. Now it is so powerful that the Bible calls the love of it the root of every kind of evil. It is known as filthy lucre or mammon, and many people place it above God himself. People will do anything for wealth. Money has a hold on the minds of many because of what they believe it can do. Money also has a spiritual component that is like a drug, and it corrupts the mind to compromise morals and values to attain it. When we resort to using the devil's tactics and schemes to acquire money, it inevitably brings forth a host of problems. Let's consider the example of winning a million-dollar jackpot through a lottery ticket. Although the winnings may seem appealing, hidden beneath the surface are unseen complications. The spiritual forces of darkness establish a legal hold on that money, attracting undesirable individuals who seek to obtain it by any means necessary. Moreover, anything we purchase with that money becomes entangled in these negative influences. Consequently, the enjoyment we anticipated is tainted, overshadowed by countless insurmountable problems.

In such instances, the true value lies in the absence of these troubles. The peace of mind and the ability to relish life's simple pleasures become immeasurably more valuable. This echoes the age-old saying that money alone does not generate happiness. It serves as a reminder that seeking fulfillment solely through material wealth often leads to undesirable consequences, whereas finding contentment in life's intangible blessings brings lasting peace and joy.

There are two kinds of prosperity mentioned in the Bible. One is based on the Babylonian world system and is purely about self-preservation and a self-centered approach. The very system encourages us to gain wealth for ourselves and store up as much as we can. It's a race to the top, and generally speaking, it is in some ways based on a system of fear about the future. We know, for example, that if one does not plan for their golden years, they might not be able to maintain the quality of life that they have grown accustomed to having. The world says to save and invest during our working years so that we will have something in our retirement. On the surface, this all seems perfectly logical.

However, have we considered what it means to truly prosper in our life in the manner that God intended it to? John writes in his third letter, 1:2, *"Beloved, I pray that in all respects you may prosper and be in good health, just as your soul prospers."* The biblical holistic vision of prosperity goes far beyond financial success. It has an effect on every facet of our lives!

How would we describe a life that is more prosperous for us? How would our lives change if we began to prosper in our relationships with the people who mean the most to us? How about spiritual success? If our spirit were flourishing with an abundance of faith, hope, and love, how might we be stronger and better able to weather life's storms? Let us learn effective strategies for experiencing prosperity in various aspects of your life. These strategies encompass relationship, spiritual, emotional, physical, financial, professional, cognitive, and social dimensions. Our goal is to shed light on the abundant resources and guidance that God has graciously provided to help you thrive in each of these areas.

The objective of this devotional is simply to begin by laying out the perspective that God has on prospering in each area, despite our desire to outline concrete steps to grow in these aspects of life. We open doors to unprecedented change and transformation when we align our perspective with His! To truly embrace prosperity, we must exhibit a willingness to submit to God's perspective as outlined in the Bible. As His beloved children, we are called to pursue this divine perspective in all areas of our lives. It is essential to recognize that prosperity extends far beyond our personal desires and ambitions; it is about equipping ourselves to lead lives that genuinely reflect and glorify God in every way.

In most of our lives, relationships are some of our greatest joys and greatest sorrows. We receive a source of life when relationships are going well! From Genesis 2:18, we know that God thinks it's bad for us to be alone. However, there are times when it seems much simpler to deal with difficulties in a relationship than to be alone.

Relationships can sometimes be absolutely heartbreaking and hurtful. However, God intends for our relationships to be sources of blessing! His Word demonstrates that He values relationships with us and is willing to endure sorrow, loss, and pain for the joy of pursuing reunification and improved relationships. His ideal vision for us is for our relationships to be fruitful and multiply in every way, uniting the lonely into families.

Spiritual prosperity depends entirely on being close to God and His Spirit! Even scientific research is beginning to acknowledge the positive effects of spiritual practices on our relationships, mental health, and spirit. According to Philippians 4:13, we have access to the ability to do "all things" through Christ, who empowers us to accomplish tasks that we would be unable to accomplish on our own. We can also have hope in our relationship with God! As we become more intimate with God and give Him the priority in our lives, our spiritual well-being improves. When we talk to God about our relationships, thoughts, and feelings, He empowers us to make changes.

Sadly, many of us have a history of prioritizing other aspects of our lives over our mental and physical well-being. When we look at Jesus, we see a person who puts a high value on the physical and emotional well-being of both Himself and His people. Jesus frequently took a break to rest His body. He humorously demonstrated in Mark 4 that a good night's sleep is more important than stress during a storm! We must believe that Jesus has the same emotional capacity as us and has experienced all of our feelings if we are to truly believe that we were created in God's image. The letter to the Hebrews tells us, *"For we do not have a high priest who is unable to sympathize with our weaknesses,"* Through them, He wants to nurture and support us! He wants our emotions to produce positive outcomes in our lives. Jesus, the Holy Spirit, and God the Father are all connected to improving our emotional well-being.

According to Deuteronomy 31:8, John 14:26, and Matthew 11:28, He can lead us out of fear and discouragement, comfort us, and provide rest when we are burdened.

"And my God will meet your every need according to His riches in glory in Christ Jesus," according to Philippians 4:19.

It would be against the Bible to avoid discussing finances; in fact, Jesus never did! Examples of God's views on money can be found in both the Old and New Testaments. The key is to keep in mind that it is a tool given to us by God to help bring heaven to Earth and accomplish His will. In heaven, we won't have to fight for finances, we won't have to live on the streets, and we won't want money. We disrespect God by rejecting God's desire for us to have enough! We can develop a positive and thriving perspective on money if we pay attention to finances in the same way that Jesus did.

Before continuing to work for God full-time, Jesus worked as a carpenter for many years. In John 5:17, Jesus said, *"My Father is always at His work, and I too am working."*

Work is a way for us to follow Christ! Our culture sometimes fails to recognize the blessings that come with work. We have been called to work by God for a reason. Scientific research has demonstrated that when we work in a healthy manner and in a healthy environment, we frequently experience improvements in our self-esteem, physical and mental health, and access to resources through connections with coworkers, clients, and other people we meet at work. Consider God's intentions and promises regarding the workplace.

In practical terms, the mind is a resource, but it can also be a disadvantage. Cognitive Behavioral Therapy (CBT) is one of the most well-liked and efficient types of therapy. According to this therapy, how we think about ourselves, the people around us, and the future determines how well we will do in life. Simply because of how we think, we sometimes limit ourselves, others, and our future unknowingly! However, God knew this prior to CBT! We are encouraged to think like Christ, to focus on things above, and to dwell on things that are beneficial and helpful (Philippians 4:8, 2 Corinthians 2:16, Colossians 3:2). Regardless of what we believe to be true if we begin replacing negative thoughts with positive ones, we can actually alter our entire life!

God, through the Trinity, exemplifies the importance of unity. In addition, the manner in which He created the world demonstrates this value. According to Romans 12:4-5 and Ephesians 4:2-3, He wants the Church to function as a united body that cooperates with one another, as says Psalm 133: *"Behold, how good and pleasant it is when brothers dwell in unity."*

In the midst of a divided world today, where suffering, resentment, and a sense of unfulfillment prevail, it is crucial to acknowledge that God holds the key to unity. By turning to Him for inspiration and guidance, we open ourselves to a transformative vision that has the power to bring about profound global change. Rather than succumbing to the challenges of division, we can seek God's wisdom and embrace His ideas, paving the way for a world united in purpose and harmony.

We learn more about God and His heart as we focus on prospering in the ways He intended!

As we embark on this journey together, let us embrace the profound truth that a relationship with Jesus serves as both the foundation and ultimate fulfillment of true prosperity. His presence in our lives illuminates the path we walk, guiding us toward abundant blessings and genuine fulfillment. Jesus is the epitome of success according to biblical teachings. He boldly announced when He arrived on Earth, *"I have come that they may have life and that they may have it more abundantly."* John 10:10 says that because He has given us access to abundance through Him. As children of God, it is our purpose to actively seek and embrace the abundance that He has bestowed upon us.

Chapter 9: God of Abundance

We had gotten everything twisted and turned in ways that God never intended when He created us. Babylon is to be blamed. Everything that was created has been corrupted by Satan, the enemy of God. According to the Bible, James 1:17, *"Every good gift and every perfect gift is from above, and comes down from the Father of lights, with whom there is no variation or shadow of turning."*

The Lord is always good, and He never varies. In order for us to be a blessing to others, He has the power to provide for each of our needs and more. He created everything for which we work under the current wage system. He is able to get us what we need when we need it. We only need to conform to His spiritual laws and maintain our faith in Him as our supply source. We are like His subjects, and God is like a King. As citizens, we adhere to the Kingdom's rules, and God's Word serves as His constitution. He will care for us through His riches in heaven if we obey Him. Citizens of the Kingdom of God are never reliant on this world's wage system. Our requirements are met by the King of Glory from a different, unrelated source.

Keep in mind that everything we see in the world is made of things we can't see. We must look to Him step by step and think with kingdom knowledge.

Consider the inspiring example of Abraham, who received a divine promise from God to become the father of many nations. Astonishingly, God spoke of this promise in the past tense, affirming, "I have made you a father of many nations." When Abraham heard this extraordinary pledge, he chose to place unwavering faith in God's Word, setting aside any doubts rooted in his own human limitations and mortality. Because Abraham listened to God, the promise is still being fulfilled. Jacob and the twelve tribes of Israel were also born from Isaac. However, when we consider the numerous individuals who continue to enter the Kingdom of God to this day, Abraham is referred to as the father of the faith in the Bible.

The unseen creates the visible, and the unseen are actual things that are kept for us in the unseen realm so that we may receive them when we put our trust in the Provider and adhere to the Kingdom's rules to obtain them. Remember that God is not preventing us from obtaining them. In God's Kingdom, only His laws and principles can work. Babylonian thinking is useless there. In moments when God is actively at work, there is an abundance that knows no limits. A particular incident involving Jesus and Peter highlights this truth. They faced a challenge when it came to paying their taxes, as was customary. Jesus provided a unique solution: He instructed them to go fishing, assuring them that the first fish they caught would hold the necessary funds. Miraculously, the first fish that emerged indeed had the money in its mouth. Recognizing the importance of maintaining a good reputation and not offending others, Jesus instructed Peter to use the money to cover their taxes.

Biblical prosperity is made possible by the grace and wisdom of the God of abundance to his Kingdom's inhabitants. These benefits are available to every true citizen, and when a blessing arrives in our lives, It's like a jar that never runs dry. Recall the incident of Elijah and the widow at Zarephath.

1 Kings 17:15-16 *"She went away and did as Elijah had told her. So there was food every day for Elijah and for the woman and her family. For the jar of flour was not used up and the jug of oil did not run dry, in keeping with the Word of the Lord spoken by Elijah."*

We move from being wage earners in the global system to citizens in His Kingdom, where all of our necessities are met without charge. When we make Jesus the Lord and Savior of our lives and learn how to use the information in His instruction manual, everything becomes possible. When it is granted by God, according to the Bible, if we pursue God's purpose on Earth and forsake everything else, He can grant us every favor, grace, and earthly blessing. In order for us to be able to help others and fulfill the calling that God has placed on our life, the Lord desires that all of our needs be met. He is the only one who can do everything, and He is waiting for His people to give up control of their lives and let Him take care of them so that He can bless them abundantly.

In John 10:10, Jesus mentioned, *"The thief comes only to steal and kill and destroy; I have come that they may have life, and have it to the full."* The Lord Jesus does not come for personal gain, unlike a thief. He comes not to take but to give. He came so that people could live meaningful, purposeful, joyful, and eternal lives in Him. When we accept Him as our Savior, we receive this abundance of life.

The Greek Word for "abundant" is "permission," which means "exceedingly, very highly, beyond measure, more, superfluous, a quantity so abundant as to be considerably more than what one would expect or anticipate." This Word comes from the Latin Word for "abundant." In a nutshell, Jesus promises us a life far superior to our wildest dreams, a concept that recalls 1

Corinthians 2:9: *"What no eye has seen, what no ear has heard, and what no human mind has conceived the things God has prepared for those who love him.* Likewise, Paul tells us in Ephesians 3:20 that God is able to do exceedingly abundantly more than we can ask or imagine. He does this through His power, which is present in us if we submit to Him.

We need to pause and consider what Jesus teaches about this abundant life before we begin to have visions of extravagant homes, pricey automobiles, world cruises, and more money than we can spend. According to the Bible, God's priorities for us are not wealth, prestige, position, or power in this world (1 Corinthians 1:26-29). While it is true that many Christians do not come from privileged social, academic, or economic backgrounds, their pursuit of an abundant life goes beyond mere material possessions. It is important to note that if wealth were the sole measure of abundance, Jesus would have been considered the wealthiest individual in history. However, a different reality is unveiled in Matthew 8:20, which presents a contrasting perspective.

In this verse, Jesus Himself declares that He does not possess a place to lay His head, indicating a lack of material possessions and earthly wealth. This highlights the fact that abundance in the context of a Christian's life encompasses a deeper meaning beyond material prosperity. It encompasses the richness of a personal relationship with God, the peace that surpasses understanding, the joy of salvation, and the fulfillment found in walking in alignment with God's purposes.

A life that begins when we accept Christ as Savior and lasts for all time is abundant life, also known as eternal life. In John 17:3, Jesus Himself provided the biblical definition of life, specifically eternal life: *"Now this is eternal life: that they know you, the only true God, and Jesus Christ, whom you have sent."* The length of a day, health, prosperity, family, and occupation are all left out of this definition. In fact, the only thing it does mention is God's knowledge, which is essential to living a truly abundant life.

What is the life of abundance? First, spiritual abundance is greater than material abundance. In point of fact, the physical circumstances of our lives do not particularly concern God. In Matthew 6:25-32, He assures us that we need not be concerned about what we eat or wear. A life centered on God may or may not include material blessings. Our standing with God is not directly proportional to our wealth or poverty. According to Ecclesiastes 5:10-15, Solomon considered all of the material blessings that a man could receive to be meaningless. Paul, on the other hand, was content regardless of his physical surroundings (Philippians 4:11–12).

Another crucial aspect to consider is that a Christian's focus on eternal life stems from their deep relationship with God rather than mere longevity. 1 John 5:11–13 tells us, "*And this is the testimony: God has given us eternal life, and this life is in his Son. Whoever has the Son has life; whoever does not have the Son of God does not have life. I write these things to you who believe in the name of the Son of God so that you may know that you have eternal life.*"

This perspective acknowledges that upon

conversion and receiving the gift of the Holy Spirit, believers already possess eternal life.

Finally, in 2 Peter 3:18, the focus of a Christian's life is to grow in the grace and knowledge of our Lord and Savior, Jesus Christ. This passage reminds us that our understanding is currently limited, similar to seeing a distorted reflection in a mirror. Therefore, abundant life entails an ongoing process of learning, practicing, maturing, and persevering As we look forward to meeting God face to face, we anticipate a time when sin and doubt will no longer hinder us. Ultimately, this will lead to a life that is abundantly fulfilled in the presence of our loving Creator.

Even though we are naturally drawn to material things, Christians must change how they see life (Romans 12:2). Our understanding of "abundance" must be altered in the same way that we become new creations when we come to Christ (2 Corinthians 5:17). According to Galatians 5:22–23, true abundant life is not characterized by an abundance of "stuff," but rather by an abundance of love, joy, peace, and the other fruits of the Spirit. It consists of eternal life, so our focus is on the eternal rather than the temporal. Colossians 3:2-3 advises us to *"Set your minds on things above, not on earthly things. For you died, and your life is now hidden with Christ in God."*

Chapter 10: Prayer

Prayer is not merely a tool to obtain our desires from God. Rather, it serves as a vital means of connecting with Him and aligning our hearts with His purposes. As followers of Jesus, prayer holds immense significance and should be approached with reverence. In this chapter, we will explore the profound importance of prayer and delve into the various ways it can positively impact our lives.

We shouldn't just pray when we go to Church or study the Bible. It's something we can do on a daily basis. As with any relationship, it will suffer if we don't spend time with that person. We can spend time with God by praying. It's a way to get in touch with Him and bring our hearts closer to Him. Through prayer, we invite God into our lives and request His direction when we pray. And if you're anything like me, I constantly require His direction!

Prayer is the single most significant activity and

the most important aspect of the Christian life. Our relationship with God is built through conversation. It fosters closeness and communion. It demonstrates God's power. Prayer answered strengthens our faith. Praying demonstrates our faith in God.

Prayer was the foundation for Jesus' entire earthly ministry. He frequently took a break from the demands of ministry to devote extended time to prayer alone. How much more ought we to live in this way if the Son of God did? We are not only required to pray when we set aside a specific time each day. Simply "Pray without ceasing" is the instruction found in 1 Thessalonians 5:17. Because, in point of fact, when do we not require prayer? "I need Thee every hour," goes the old hymn. Through Christ, we always have access to the grace throne; We only need to scream.

Prayers don't always get answered the way we want. Paul described a period in his life when he had a thorn in his flesh, but he didn't say what it was. He also said that *"Three times I pleaded with the Lord about this, that it should leave me,"* 2 Cor. 12:7-9. However, God's response is not to remove this "thorn" but rather to provide us with what we require, as shown in the following verse. *"But he said to me, My grace is sufficient for you, for my power is made perfect in weakness. "*. God does not eliminate every challenge, and neither does He provide everything that our fleshly selves believe we ought to have. He gives us a lot of His grace, and we don't need anything else to get through the hardest, darkest times in life.

One of the people I look up to for prayer has a good way of combining reading God's Word with long, scattered prayers. She stops reading and prays whenever God reminds her of something or writes someone on her heart. She prays during her time in the Word. What a beautiful combination of the two most essential aspects of the Christian life, and what a transformation each believer—and the Church as a whole—would undergo if they began their mornings in a similar manner!

We must evaluate our prayer life for a few moments. How does it appear? Is it time spent at God's throne, enjoying precious moments of communion with

Him, or is it more like a cry for help spoken after our own resources have run out? Let us be honest and ourselves, "Who do we confide in when we are feeling down, and to whom do we turn when life seems to be taking over? Is Jesus Christ the rock on which we stand and our life's anchor? We cannot be strengthened by anyone else, and nothing else will satisfy us.

Even though we should always seek out uninterrupted time for this spiritual discipline, daily prayer may not always work. The beauty of walking with God is that we can do it anywhere, whether we are doing housework, running errands, studying, or just hanging out with friends. There are many opportunities to pray instead of thinking about nothing. God is always with us and ready to listen.

No matter where they are right now, the majority of people want to see their finances improve. We always strive for improvement, especially during our working years. An interesting fact is that it is our duty to safeguard what God has provided for us. We need to keep our lives safe from bad decisions, problems that aren't needed, and bad people. We may frequently receive incorrect advice. For example, God told Adam to keep the Garden of Eden safe from the enemy, but unfortunately, he followed Eve's lead and lost everything.

Prayer serves as a means to safeguard and preserve the blessings bestowed upon us by God. Through prayer, we create an atmosphere of divine protection for our families and possessions. Additionally, prayer enhances our receptivity to God's specific guidance, allowing us to be more attuned to spiritual matters.

One biblical example that illustrates the concept of prayer as a means of divine protection is found in the book of Psalms, specifically in Psalm 91. This psalm is often referred to as the "Psalm of Protection" or the "Prayer of Safety."

"Whoever dwells in the shelter of the Most High will rest in the shadow of the Almighty. I will say of the LORD, 'He is my refuge and my fortress, my God, in whom I trust.'"

The psalm continues to describe how God's faithful ones are shielded from harm, danger, and various forms of destruction.

God wants to talk to us every day, and He does talk more than we think. In order to hear that distinct voice attempting to direct us, everyone needs to be on the right frequency.

We rely on the Holy Spirit to enable us to discern His voice, and when we do, we must promptly obey. By doing so, we develop a mindset aligned with the values of God's Kingdom and let go of worldly perspectives influenced by Babylon. He wants to assist us in seeing His best for our life, including the decisions we make every day. God can even assist us in making better financial decisions that will increase our supply of everything we require. Our finances will be shielded by the Lord from the evil forces that come to kill, steal, and destroy. The devil would love to control our financial decisions so that we will never be able to serve God and lose our money. We can avoid a lot of problems by consulting God about upcoming decisions or commitments.

When engaging in prayer, it is important to be mindful of the individuals we allow into our inner circle. We should exercise discernment when granting access to our lives. In our journey, there are those who deposit positivity and support, while others tend to drain and deplete us. It can be said that God strategically places certain individuals in our lives to bring blessings. Some people are contributors, offering their own resources and adding value to our lives. They uplift and benefit us rather than being a burden.

God can assist us in a wide range of matters, such as choosing insurance that will ultimately save money. Choosing the right house for us and our family is another example. When we are ready to retire, God may have us purchase in a location where the value of our home will have significantly increased in ten years. We would never be able to know things that God has for us without a life of obedience. That knowledge and the benefits can be ours when we delegate its care to Him.

Another aspect of prayer that is frequently

overlooked is the spiritual power that prayer gives us to resist following our own paths. When we want something, the devil frequently uses it to steer us in the opposite direction of God. We feel compelled by our natural desire to have whatever it is that we want, despite our inhibitions about going in a different direction. According to the Bible, we have an inclination towards the lust of the flesh, lust of the eyes, and the pride of life rather than allowing our spirit nature to rule.

Every day, our soul wrestles for control, but by investing time in our relationship with God, we nurture our spiritual growth and become victorious overcomers. Prioritizing our spiritual nature over our earthly desires empowers us to make wiser decisions. Maintaining an open line of communication with God through frequent prayer is essential, guarding it against anything that could hinder it. Additionally, cultivating intimacy with God aligns with the biblical recommendation for our relationship with Him. Consistent prayer enables God to reveal His perfect will for our lives. When we step out in faith based on His guidance, we witness the manifestation of His promises. God faithfully meets our needs and fulfills the vision He has placed within us for His glory.

www.ingramcontent.com/pod-product-compliance
Lightning Source LLC
Chambersburg PA
CBHW071018120626
46546CB00003B/1141